A Professional Guide to

iPhone 12

Cameras

For the Elderly

(Large Print Edition)

A Step by Step Approach to Taking Professional
Photographs and shooting Cinematic Videos on the
iPhone 12 Pro and 12 Pro Max

DERRICK
RICHARD

Copyright

Derrick Richard
ChurchGate Publishing House
USA | UK | Canada
© Churchgate Publishing House 2020

Contents

Copyright..i

CHAPTER ONE.. **1**

UNLEASHING THE iPhone 12 CAMERA CAPABILITIES 1

Get quick access to your iPhone 12 camera 2

Use the iPhone Control Center... 3

Add your camera application to the Dock.......................... 3

Take Your Shot in Multiple Ways 4

Enable the Grid Guides... 6

Shoot in Burst Mode.. 7

Set Up Manual Focus and Exposure..................................... 8

Take HDR Photos..11

Turn off automatic HDR..12

How to quickly Access Different Photo Types 13

Take a Live Photo 14

How to play a live photo..15

Editing a live photo...16

Take a panorama photo...18

How to use iPhone portrait mode to take amazing
portrait photos... 23

How to change the level of blur with the Depth.................26

How to use the depth control..26

Take a photo with a filter...28

Take low-light photos with Night mode...........................28

Take videos with your iPhone 12 camera........................30

Record a video...30

Use quick toggles to change video resolution and
frame rate... 32

Change Aspect ratio...33

Record a QuickTake video...34

How to shoot a slow motion video on iPhone.................35

How to convert slow motion video into a normal
regular video on your device... 36

How to convert your normal video to the slow motion
video... 37

Speeding up or slowing down a slo-mo video on your
device... 38

How to deploy a third-party app to make your video go
slower or faster.. 39

CHAPTER TWO 41

THE PHOTO APP: EXTENDING CAMERA
CAPABILITIES.. 41

View photos and videos on iPhone..................................41

Browse photos..42

Edit Live Photos on iPhone..44

Edit a Live Photo 44

Add effects to a Live Photo 45

Play a Live Photo 46

Play a video 46

Play and customize a slideshow 47

Delete and hide photos and videos on iPhone 47

Delete or hide a photo or video 48

Recover or permanently delete deleted photos 49

Organize photos in albums on iPhone 12 50

Add photos and videos to existing albums 51

How to remove photos and videos from your existing
albums 52

How to rearrange, rename, and delete your existing
albums 53

How to sort photos in albums 53

How to filter photos in your albums 54

Organize albums in folders 54

Share photos and videos on iPhone 55

Share photos with Sharing Suggestions 57

Save or share a photo or video you receive 59

CHAPTER THREE **60**

TECHNIQUES FOR RETOUCHING YOUR PHOTOS **60**

Fix a Photo's Colors 61

Modify Colors Using the Photos App...............................62

Remove Photo Casting..64

Make a Color Adjustment Using Adobe Lightroom...........66

Panel in Loupe view 67

Edit panel 68

Apply Selective Edit..68

How to remove unnecessary spots and any unwanted
objects in your picture... 77

Crop photos..81

Working with preset on your photo...................................83

How to Apply Presets..83

How to create preset for a user 84

How to delete or update a user preset...............................87

How to manage presets 89

How to hide presets that are partially compatible............90

Adjust the tonal scale of a photo 92

How to Fine-tune the tonal scale using the Tone Curve ..95

How to adjust color in your image 96

How to apply effects in your images 99

How to use Noise reduction to get your photos
sharpened...101

How to correct common camera lens flaws...................... 104

How to Copy and paste edits 105

How to create edit version 108

How to send your photos to Photoshop on iPad............. 111

CHAPTER FOUR **113**

HANDY PHOTOGRAPHY AND VIDEO ACCESSORIES FOR THE iPhone 12 .... **113**

iPhone photo editing software 126

CHAPTER FIVE **129**

FilMic Pro App for Cinematic video: Getting more than just a video **129**

How to set Focus using the FilMic Pro.................... 130

How to set Resolution in FilMic Pro 132

How to choose Aspect ratio..................................... 134

How to adjust frame rate on FilMic Pro 136

How to adjust Video exposure in FilMic Pro......... 139

Setting white balance... 143

Recording Videos on the FilMic Pro 144

Device Settings... 145

ABOUT AUTHOR... **147**

CHAPTER ONE

UNLEASHING THE iPhone 12 CAMERA CAPABILITIES

There is no gainsaying that good photo-graphy requires both the skills of the photographer and the power of the camera. With your iPhone 12 camera, you will be able to take photo and videos for both profess-ional and personal purposes. To get the maximum benefit from your iPhone camera, it is important you understand your camera capabilities and all of the beautiful features that will contribute to improved shot you can always get from your phone camera. This chapter will show you some basic features of the iPhone camera and the Photo App on your iPhone before going deep into the different ways of enhancing your videos and photos in the subsequent chapters.

Get quick access to your iPhone 12 camera

The ability to take pictures and record videos anywhere and at any time is one of the iPhone's intriguing capabilities. For instance, how better can you quickly record a video of your baby taking his/her first step to walk or snap pictures from your vacation on an island without using the camera feature on your phone? All that you basically have to do is take out your iPhone 12, launch your camera application and begin to take amazing shots already. However, in order to quickly capture those great moments instantly, you will need to understand how and where to access your camera app from. With your iPhone 12, the following are easy ways of launching your camera;

Swipe to Open

This method involves swiping through your phone screen. This enables you to utilize your Camera application even while your device is locked, which is perhaps the quickest way to access your device's camera;

1. If the iPhone 12 is asleep, simply press the side button to wake it up. Your iPhone 12 does not have a sleep/wake button at the top of your device, but it has a side button that can be used to wake it.

2. From the lock screen, swipe left or touch and then hold 📷, then remove your finger.

Use the iPhone Control Center

Launch the iPhone Control Center by simply swiping down from the top-right edge of your screen. From the list of available option, simply locate your camera app and click on it.

Add your camera application to the Dock

The Dock is located at the lower end of the main screen. To add your camera app to the Dock;

- Navigate to your device home screen to access the various apps.
- Tap and then hold lightly on the icon of your Camera app until your camera app

begins to jiggle. The jiggling motion is telling you that the camera app is ready to be dragged to a new location.

- Drag the camera app to your screen dock next to the apps you most frequently used such as the Safari browser and the Mail app. In case the Dock is already full with app, quickly hold on an app you don't used frequently and remove such app from the Dock to accommodate the camera app on the Dock.

Take Your Shot in Multiple Ways

The iPhone allows users to snap your pictures using three different means based essentially on different situations. The default method is by tapping on your Camera button once to snap the picture as shown in the image below.

You can as well press your iPhone volume up button or volume down button to snap the picture as displayed in the image below. With this option, you will be able to hold your iPhone 12 properly while snapping the pictures. This works the same way like the shutter button on your digital camera (for professional photographer using digital camera) if your device is in landscape mode. Finally, if you have a wired headset, the volume buttons on the headset can be deployed to snap the shot. This allows you to stealthily snap your photos. For instance, you will be able to capture good moments of friends at a party without them noticing to get some spontaneous pictures. You will be able to avoid shaking your device while taking your pictures when you used the headset buttons to snap your shot.

Enable the Grid Guides

As most professional photographers under-stand, the composition of any photo is one of the factors that inform an amazing shot. Your camera app provides grids that can help you while you are taking your shot to make sure the composition of your shot is naturally appealing. With the grid option, you will be able to divide your screen into three different columns and rows. The Grid helps you to straighten your shot. To activate the Grid feature on your device, proceed with the steps below;

- Navigate to the **Settings app** on your device.
- Move down the settings and click on "**Photo & Camera**."
- Toggle on the **Grid** feature in your camera section as shown below;

After you snap a picture, you can deploy the editing tools in your Photos app to help align your shots and also adjust the horizontal and vertical perspective.

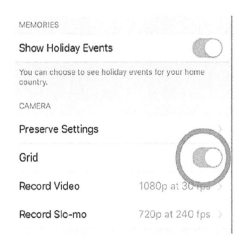

MEMORIES

Show Holiday Events

You can choose to see holiday events for your home country.

CAMERA

Preserve Settings

Grid

Record Video   1080p at 30 fps >

Record Slo-mo   720p at 240 fps >

Shoot in Burst Mode

For events that are happening fast like sports or children dancing at a party, you may want to snap multiple shots of the event to allow you to select the best picture later.

While tapping on your camera button repeatedly might be too slow, your iPhone's Burst mode can be used. With the burst mode, you can snap multiple images almost immed-iately by taping and holding on your device's camera button. More pictures can be taken in burst mode by holding the button longer. Once the button has been released, your photos will be saved in a folder called Burst folder in the Camera roll. Follow the steps below to access pictures in burst folder;

1. In your Photos app, click on the Burst folder to choose it.
2. Click on "Select" in the middle-bottom toolbar.
3. You can then explore the various photos in burst set.

To see one picture in the folder, do these;

1. Click on the image and then tap "**Done**" located at the top right of your screen.
2. You can either tap "**Keep Everything**" to keep your folder and save the choose image (or images) as a separate image or select "**Keep One.**"

Set Up Manual Focus and Exposure

By default, your iPhone camera will automatically set the focus in your picture toward the nearest object in the composition. Nonetheless, you can still change this setting; for instance, you might need to focus on a far item in your shot. The iPhone 12 camera will give you option to set the focus and exposure of your picture by tapping on the item that you your camera to focus on and your camera will shift its focus to the object you selected. See the image below;

Adjust the camera's focus and exposure

Before you start taking photos on your device, your iPhone camera automatically adjusts the focus and exposure, and the face detection will balance the exposure across many faces. To adjust the focus and exposure manually, you can do the following settings;

1. Tap on your screen to display the automatic focus area and the exposure setting.

2. Tap anywhere you wish to move the focus area.

3. Drag the ☀ up or down next to the focus area to adjust your exposure.

Lock the Exposure and Focus

Although, your iPhone 12 camera provides you with the flexibility of setting the exposure and the focus in your shot, it still has a drawback, most especially when you are snapping a picture where the item may move. Or you might wish to snap multiple images of the same screen each time you take your shot without necessarily changing the focus.

To lock the exposure settings and manual focus for your upcoming shots, touch and then hold the camera focus area until you see the **AE/AF lock;** then tap your screen to unlock settings. You will be able to precisely set and lock exposure for your upcoming shots by tapping on ⌃ and then tap ± while moving the slider to adjust exposure settings. The exposure will lock until when you launch the camera. To preserve your exposure control so that it is not automatically reset when you launch Camera, navigate to **Settings** , tap on **Camera**, select "**Preserve Settings,**" and then enable (turn it on) the "**Exposure Adjustment.**"

Take HDR Photos

High dynamic range (HDR) photos are a mixture of images of the same shot recorded using different exposure values. A dramatic effect known as **HDR photo effect** is created in the image by merging between these photos. Unlike the normal pictures, HDR photos feature more contrasting colors and variations of light and shades. The iPhone 12 camera is able to automatically take pictures in HDR, though you can adjust this setting by turning off the automatic HDR feature. Be aware that shooting photos of moving items with this technique may result in distorted images since the features allows you to snap three images with different exposures and then merge them together. So, it is actually best to deploy this feature with still items/subjects.

Turn off automatic HDR

By default, your iPhone 12 camera automatically deploys the HDR mode when it is most effective. If you want to control HDR manually;

- On your iPhone 12, navigate to **Settings**, tap on **Camera**, and then disable "**Smart HDR.**" Then from your camera screen, tap on HDR to turn it on/off.

Turn HDR video off and on

Your iPhone normally takes video in Dolby Vision HDR to achieve true-to-life color and contrast. You can disable the HDR video recording by navigating to **Settings**, tap on

"**Camera,**" click on "**Record Video**," and then disable HDR Video.

How to quickly Access Different Photo Types

You can leverage on the iPhone 12 camera to snap varieties of photos including slo-mo, portrait, video, panorama etc. The default method you can use to switch between these photo modes is to launch your camera and swipe right or left on your camera modes at the end of your camera screen. There are many ways to access the camera on your device. From the lock screen, simply tap and hold firmly on the camera app to bring the quick action menu as shown below;

Take a Live Photo

You will be able to capture what is going on in the background just before you snap your picture and right after the picture must have been taken, including the sounds. Literally, you can record movements in your pictures with the live photo mode rather than freezing a moment with the still photo. The live photo will capture about 3 seconds movement in your image, for instance about 1.5 seconds of motion is captured right before you tap on your camera's shutter button and about 1.5 seconds will be captured again once you tap on your camera's shutter button.

To take a live photo;

1. Choose the "Photo mode" among the list of camera modes at the lower end of your camera screen.

2. Tap on ⊚ at the top section of your camera screen to enable/disable Live Photos.

3. Capture the picture by clicking on your camera's shutter button.

How to play a live photo

Once you have successfully taken a live photo, it will be saved in your Photo app together with other still photos you have taken. But it is difficult to know whether an image is actually a live photo or not if you are viewing the list of images in thumbnail view. For instance, look at the image below and see if you can tell which of the image is actually a live photo and which one is not.

Obviously, it will be difficult to tell exactly which of the images above is really a live photo and which is not. One simple trick you can use to know which one is a live photo is by tapping on an image to open such image in full screen. If the picture is actually a live photo, the word **live** will appear at the top section of your screen as shown below;

Editing a live photo

If you desire to edit a particular live photo, simply open the picture and click on the **edit** menu at the top right side of your camera's screen and you will see the editing tools at the bottom of your screen;

Select the **adjust** icon to adjust color, sharpness and exposure for the image by using a range of tools that will be provided.

You can swipe from right to left and vice versa to choose between different adjustment tools. Once you have chosen the tool you want, you can then drag the slider to effect the adjustment.

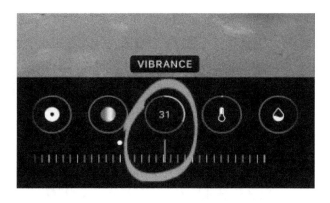

Use the **Filter** icon to apply color. Swipe between each filter and then apply the one you want to see the change.

Use the **Crop** icon to crop or to rotate the photo.

During cropping, you can straighten your picture by tapping on the **straighten** icon and then drag the slider to the left or right;

For proper cropping of your picture, you will have four corner crop handles that you can drag;

The icons at the top left of the screen can be used to rotate/flip your picture;

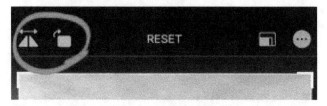

Take a panorama photo

A panoramic photo is one that is wider than it is taller. With this photo mode, you can cover all of your friends in one click. The only thing that will be sacrificed is the height of the picture. Panoramas provide a good means of shooting shots, which are rather too wide or tall to fit into the camera viewfinder. The Panorama mode can be used to snap land-scapes or any other pictures that will not ordinarily fit on your camera screen. To do this;

1. Choose Pano mode from the photo mode at the lower end of your camera screen and click on the shutter button of your device camera.

2. Slowly pan in the arrow's direction, while still maintain-ing the arrow on the center line.

3. Click on the shutter button of your device's camera.

To create a professional panorama photo, consider the following tips and tricks;

- **Open Pano Mode**

Click on your camera app from your device home screen to launch the iPhone camera. Swipe from left to right to select between different shooting mode until you see pano mode in display.

- **Carry out a test run of your shot.**

It is good to carry out a "pre-run" of your photo to see how the final image will look like. Hold your camera upright in portrait mode to create a horizontal panorama. You can then begin to pan your camera from right to left and vice versa across your scene while keeping in mind the area you want the photo to start and end.

- **Lock Exposure**

One important thing, when you are considering shooting panorama picture, is setting the exposure correctly. Your iPhone camera is able to choose its exposure according to how bright or dark the scene looks at the beginning of the panoramic shot. If the beginning of your shot is much lighter or darker than the remaining part of the scene, the end result will be that some parts of the picture will be over-exposed or under-exposed. What you are actually looking for here is a part of your scene that is not too light or too dark– this is the area that will give you a balanced exposure. Once you have seen an area of moderate brightness, simply point your device at it, then tap on the screen, and hold at that exact point. Doing this will lock the exposure for the rest of the panorama shot.

- **Set The Panning Direction**

In case you plan to begin the panoramic shot from your left, make sure that the arrow is actually pointing to your right. In the same vein, if you plan to begin your panoramic shot from the right, make sure that the arrow is actually pointing to your left. In case that arrow is pointing in the wrong direction, you can tap on the arrow to make it switch direction.

- **Shoot Your Panorama**

To create your panorama picture, let your device point at the starting point of your panoramic photo and then press your camera's shutter button to begin shooting. You can then pan your device slowly toward the end position.

Ensure that you don't stop moving and that you maintain the arrow on the displayed line. The device will inform you once you have too far from that line – or once you are going too fast.

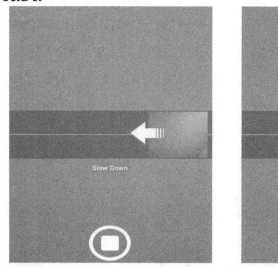 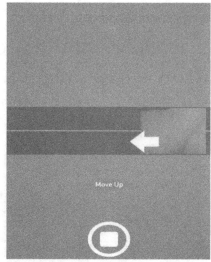

Once the end position has been reached, you can then terminate shooting either by pressing your camera's shutter button once more or by just reversing the panning through moving the camera back a short distance in the opposite direction. The later method is okay as you can avoid shaking your iPhone camera while still maintaining your hands position. You should keep panning until your iPhone stops automatically. With this, you have created a professional panorama picture and you can go ahead to view the picture in the photo App.

How to use iPhone portrait mode to take amazing portrait photos

Portrait mode is one of the shooting modes in your camera with ability to blur backgrounds that are not necessary in your picture.

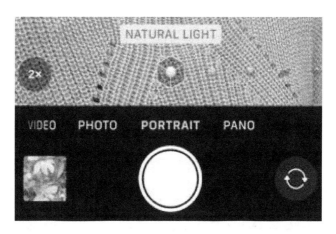

With the Portrait mode, taking professional portrait picture is nothing but easy. The face of the subject (the person or subject you want to snap) will be very sharp while the background remains blurred.

With a blurred background, the subject will really stand out while emphasizing the look of the subject. The portrait mode is useful – especially – with a busy or not so attractive background. The background will still show but it will be blurry and the attention of the people viewing your photo will be drawn to the subject that is the main purpose of the picture.

To use the portrait mode, launch the Camera app and swipe through the various shooting modes at the bottom of the camera screen to have the Portrait mode.

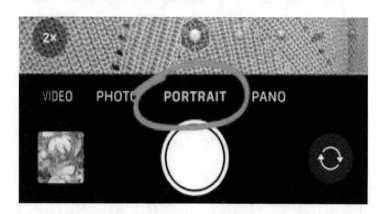

While using the portrait mode, some important tips that you can consider include;

Do not shoot the portrait mode in a low light situation. If the light is not enough, the camera app will give you a message that you require more light to use the portrait mode.

Also, the subject must be between two to eight feet away from your camera. If your subject is actually too close or even too far away, you will be asked to draw closer or to move further away. When you have positioned yourself at the right distance from the subject, the word "Natural Light" will appear in yellow.

This shows that your device has successfully identified your subject and its background.

The camera can then focus automatically on the face of your subject and then proceed to blur out its background. Once the shot has been properly composed, simply click on your camera's shutter button to take the picture. The picture you get will be very beautiful portrait image that has a blurred background that looks dreamy.

Once you have successfully taken your picture, the level of blur in the background can be adjusted. You can as well proceed to add studio effect or eliminate the blur completely.

How to change the level of blur with the

Depth

The **Depth Control** feature on your device will allow you to adjust the strength of the blur in your picture's background right after you have successfully snapped a photo.

How to use the depth control

From your **photo app,** click on a picture to see the picture in portrait mode, and then select **Edit** from the top right side of your screen.

Click on the f/number icon located at the top left side of your screen.

The Depth slider will appear below your picture. Simply drag the Depth slider to the right or left to make your background blur weaker or stronger.

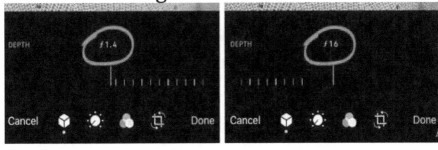

The smaller the chosen f/number, the blurrier your background appears. In the picture above, f/1.4 will give a very blurry background, while the f/16 will bring more detail in the background. When you have successfully chosen the amount of background you want, simply click on "Done" to finish. The strength of the blur can be changed anytime you want by opening the Edit option once more.

Take a photo with a filter

Choose portrait mode or Photo, tap on ⌃ , and then click ⬤ .

Below the viewer, swipe the filters to the right or left to preview the filter and then click on one of them to choose.

Take low-light photos with Night mode

On your iPhone, the Night mode will allow you to capture more information and then brighten your shots when you are in a low light situation. Although, the length of the exposure in the Night mode is determined automatically, but there is a way you can manually adjust the length.

On your iPhone 12, the Night mode is found on your phone's front camera for selfie, on your Ultra Wide (0.5x) camera, and also on your Wide (1x) camera.

1. Select Photo mode. In a low-light situation, the Night mode will turn on automatically: you will see the ⊜ button at the top of your screen turning yellow and there will be a number next to the ⊜ button to show how many seconds your phone camera will take to capture.

2. You can experiment with the Night mode by clicking on ⊜ and then deploy the slider just below the frame to choose between the Max and Auto timers. With Auto timers, the time will be determined automatically, while the Max uses the longest time. The setting you make here will be preserved for the next Night mode shot

3. Click on your camera's shutter button and then hold the camera still to take your shot.

   You will see crosshairs in the frame if the iPhone notices movement during capture— you can actually align the crosshairs if you wish to limit motions and improve the quality of your shot.

To stop capturing a Night mode shot midway, simply tap on the Stop button located below the slider.

Take videos with your iPhone 12 camera

Aside from taking mouthwatering pictures with your camera, the camera app 📷 can also be used to take clear cinematic videos that can be uploaded on your YouTube channel and other social media platforms.

Record a video

1. Swipe through the list of shooting mode at the bottom of the camera screen and select Video mode.

2. Tap on the Record button or you can alternatively press either the volume up or volume down button to initiate recording. You will still be able to do the following while you are recording a video;

   • Take a still picture by tapping on the white Shutter button.

- Pinch the screen to zoom in and out on the screen.

- To get a more define zoom, touch and then hold the 1x while adjusting the slider to the left.

To stop recording, tap on the camera record button or you can alternatively use either the volume down or volume up button.

Videos recorded with your device normally record at 30 frame rate per seconds (fps). You will be able to choose from other frame rate by scrolling to **Settings,** click on **Camera** and choose "**Record Video.**" It is obvious that the faster the frame per seconds and the large the resolution, the larger the video file will be.

You can use multiple microphones to achieve stereo sound on your iPhone. To disable Stereo recording, go to **Settings** ," click on "Camera," and then disable Record Stereo Sound.

The iPhone 12 will normally shoot videos in HDR and can as well share the same video with other users using devices running on iOS

13.4, macOS 10.15.4 and iPadOS 13.4; while most other devices will get the same video as an SDR version. You can deactivate the HDR recording by navigating to **Settings**, click on "**Camera,**" choose "**Record Video**," and then disable the HDR Video.

Use quick toggles to change video resolution and frame rate

In Video mode, you can use the quick toggles found at the top section of the screen to change your video resolution and frame rates.

On your camera app, click on the quick toggles found at the top-right side to work between the 4K or HD mode and 60, 30, or 24 frames per second (fps) in the Video mode.

Change Aspect ratio

Launch your Camera app and click on the arrow found on the action bar at the top. This arrow will bring some buttons in the action bar at the bottom just above the shutter button. Simply tap on the 4:3 icon, and choose the aspect ratio you want.

Record a QuickTake video

You recorded this video in Photo mode. You will still be able to adjust the video's record button into a lock position to keep capturing still pictures while you are making a Quick-Take video.

1. In the Photo mode, simply touch and then hold your Camera's Shutter button to initiate taking a QuickTake video.

2. Perform a hands-free recording by sliding the camera's shutter button to your right side and leave the lock. The shutter button and the record button will be shown below the frame.

3. To stop recording, tap on the Record button.

Tip: Press and then hold either the volume increase or volume decrease button to begin to take a QuickTake video in Photo mode. Tap on the thumbnail to access the QuickTake video in your Photos app.

How to shoot a slow motion video on iPhone

Recording a slo-mo video with your device camera implies slowing down the frame rate so that the time will now appear to be moving at a rather slow rate within your video. Filmmakers use this effect to achieve a unique video of nature scenes, athletic footage or scenes that has lot of actions/events that are intense. To do a slo-mo video using the camera of your iPhone 12, follow the steps below;

1. From the home screen of your device, open your camera app by tapping on the app icon.
2. Activate the slo-mo (turn on the slo-mo feature) by tapping on slo-mo. Record in

slow-motion on iPhone 12 with your front camera by tapping on .

3. Click on the red Record button or use either of the volume buttons to initiate recording.

4. Tap the shutter button once again to cease recording.

5. Go to the Photos app on your phone to access the new slow motion video.

How to convert slow motion video into a

normal regular video on your device

You can deploy the Photo App on your device to turn the slo-mo video clip into a normal regular video. This is possible especially when you mistakenly recorded the video in slo-mo or you just decided to produce the video in real time. To do this;

1. Launch the Photos app and go to the slow motion recording that you plan to speed up.

2. At the lower end of your screen, there is a slider indicating where the video switches from normal speed to the slow motion speed. Simply drag the small white line just on the left across the slider till you completely change all of the slo-mo areas to regular speed.

3. Move the slider in either direction to get rid of the slow motion effect or to get rid of small part of the slo-mo video.

4. Tap on "**Done**" when you are okay with the result.

How to convert your normal video to the slow motion video

The iMovie app can be used to convert a video that was shot normally to a slo-mo video. To do this;

1. Launch the iMovie app and click on the + icon to begin a new project with your video.

2. Click on "Edit" to access the edit screen.

3. On the editing interface, simply hold down on the area of your video that you wish to slow down. If you desire to slow down the whole video, simply use your finger to drag across the entire timeline until you see it highlighted/marked in yellow.

4. Click on the icon that looks like a wheel (speed adjustment icon) on the lower end of your screen. The speed adjustment icon actually looks like a car speedometer.

5. You can then drag your finger across the slider to select the speed for the video clip. You can decide to use one-eight or you can just decide to double the video's current speed.

6. Click on **Play** to watch the video, and when the result is okay, tap on "**Done.**"

Speeding up or slowing down a slo-mo video

on your device

The methods outlined above can be used to increase or reduce the rate at which your video is playing by deploying the iMovie app. However, you will not have the leverage to let the slow motion part of the video clip to be slower than your device's frame rate capability.

When you access a slo-mo video from the iMovie app, you will be able to access where the video clip begins to slow down right at the lower end of the timeline. If you place your finger on the exact part that you wish to change, the speed slider will display how fast or slow the video is playing. If the slo-mo video is already playing at one-eighth speed, slowing it down further will be difficult. However, you can still speed up the video by navigating your finger to the right side on the speed slider.

How to deploy a third-party app to make your video go slower or faster

Although, the iMovie app gives you a practical way of speeding up or slowing your videos using the iMovie app, it still has some limitations. To have advanced control over the speed of any video on your iPhone, you can try a third party app such as <u>Slow Fast Motion Video Editor</u>, which you can get on the App Store.

Using the Slow & Fast app, slowing down part of a video while speeding up others is possible. You will also be able to trim the video into clips. Then, for each clip, select from −8x to +8x speeds. This gives a rather simple and excellent way to get your slo-mo videos faster or slower than what you can get with your Camera app.

CHAPTER TWO

THE PHOTO APP: EXTENDING CAMERA CAPABILITIES

View photos and videos on iPhone

The Photos app on your device can be deployed to navigate your videos and photos organized by days, months, years, and all photos. Click on the "Albums," "For You," and "Search" tabs to navigate photos sorted out by different categories and also to create albums that can be shared to other people.

- *Library:* Navigate your videos and photos sorted out by years, months and days.

- *For You:* Show your shared albums, memories, featured photos and a lot more.

- *Albums:* See albums you shared or created, and your pictures sorted by album categories—for instance, Media Types and People & Places.

- *Search:* Use the search bar to look for pictures by location, objects they contain, date, or caption. You will also be able to view images that have been grouped already by important places, people and categories.

Tap to view full screen.

Browse photos

The images and videos on your device are usually organized by **All Photos**, **Years, Months**, and **Days in the Library tab**. You can find your best pictures in Years, access notable events in Months, view unique photos in Days, and access everything all together in All Photos.

Click on the Library tab to browse your images, and then select any of the following:

- Years: Quickly find a specific year in the photo library, and view significant events marked in a slideshow.

- Months: Access collections of images that you shot throughout the month, organized by important events—like a social gathering, family outing, trip or marriage ceremony.

- Days: See your lovely photos in chronological order, where they will be grouped by the exact place and time you took them.

- All Photos: Access all of your videos and photos at a glance. You can also zoom in or out on the photo, view the photos by square or aspect ratio, filter the photo and view photo on map by tapping on located at the top of the photo screen.

Edit Live Photos on iPhone

Use your Photos app ✿ to edit Live Photos, add some fun effects like Loop and Bounce and change the Key Photo.

Edit a Live Photo

Adding filters or cropping a video is not the only editing you can do to a live photo, as you can edit a live photo by trimming the length of the photo, changing the key photo and muting the sound.

1. Open a Live Photo and select "Edit."

2. Tap ◎, then do any of the following:

- **Set a key photo:** Simply move the frame that looks like white square and select "Make key photo" shown at the top of the white frame.

- **Trim a Live Photo:** You can select the frames you want the live photo by dragging any of the two ends of the frame viewer.

- **Make a still photo:** Click on the Live button located at the top area of the screen to disable (turn off) the Live feature. The Live Photo will turn to a still photo.

- **Mute a Live Photo:** Tap on the mute icon located at the top section of the screen. To un-mute, tap on the icon again.

Add effects to a Live Photo

Live Photos can be turn into fun videos by adding effects to the photos.

1. Open a Live Photo.

2. Swipe up on the photo screen to bring the effects below the image, and then select from one of the following:

   - Loop: This effect will repeat the action in a continuous looping video.

   - Bounce: This effect will carry out a rewind action backward and forward.

- Long Exposure: This effect will simulates a DSLR-like long exposure effect by blurring motion.

Play a Live Photo

A Live Photo ◎ is any moving image that records those moments right before and just after a picture is shot.

1. Open the Live Photo.

2. Touch the video and hold on it to play the video.

Play a video

The videos you have in your library automatically auto-play while you scroll and browse through your photos in the Library tab. Click on a video to play such video in full screen without any sound. You can do any of these;

- Click on the player controls right below the video to play, mute, unmute and pause the video. Tap on the video screen to hide the player control.

- You can also double-tap the video screen if you want to toggle between the fit-to-screen and the full screen mode.

Play and customize a slideshow

A collection of your images that has been formatted and set to music is called Slideshow.

1. Click on the Library tab.

2. Access your photos by "Days" or "All Photos" and then choose "Select."

3. Select each image that you wish to add in the slideshow and then click on ⬆️.

4. Select **"Slideshow"** from the list of options.

5. Tap on the screen, then select "Options" from the bottom right to change the slideshow music, theme, and more.

Delete and hide photos and videos on iPhone

In your Photos app 🌸, you will be able to delete videos and photos from your device or even hide them in the Hidden album. Recently deleted photos can also be recovered. With iCloud Photos, any changes you edited will be saved across all of your devices sharing the same iCloud account.

Delete or hide a photo or video

In Photos, select a video or photo, and then proceed to carry out either of the following:

- **Delete:** Click on 🗑 to remove a photo or video from your device and from all of your devices sharing the same iCloud Photo logins.

  Any video or pictures you deleted will be saved in the "Recently Deleted" album for a period of 30 days. Within this period, you can decide to decide to recover them or even delete them permanently delete them from all of your devices.

- **Hide:** Click on ⬆ and then select "Hide" from the list of options.

  Any photo you hide from view will be moved to an album called Hidden album.

You will not be able to access them anywhere else.

If you want to turn off the Hidden album so that it will not appear in Albums,

navigate to **Settings** ⚙, tap on "**Photos**," and then proceed to turn off Hidden Album.

Recover or permanently delete deleted photos

If you want to recover pictures that you have deleted or to delete a photo permanently, proceed with the following steps;

1. Navigate to the Albums tab and then click on "Recently Deleted" located under "Utilities."

2. Click on "Select," and then select the videos and photos that you wish to delete or recover.

3. Select "Recover" or "Delete" at the bottom of the camera screen.

Organize photos in albums on iPhone 12

Organize your images with album by using the Photos app . Click on the Albums tab to view albums you created, albums that were created automatically and shared Albums you joined or created.

People & Places

Library   For You   Albums   Search

With iCloud Photos, your albums will be saved in iCloud. iCloud albums are up to date and will be accessible on devices where you are signed in with the same Apple ID and password.

Create an album

Organize your pictures by creating albums.

1. In Photos, click on the Albums tab and then select +.

2. Choose between creating a New album or a New Shared Album.

3. Enter a suitable name for the album, and then select "Save."

4. Tap all of the photos that you want to add in the album and select "Done."

Add photos and videos to existing albums

1. At the lower end of the screen, click on the Library tab and then choose "select."

2. Tap on the photo and the thumbnails of the video that you want to add, and then select ⬆️

3. Swipe up in the screen, and then choose "Add to Album" from the list of actions.

4. Select the album that you wish to add to.

How to remove photos and videos from your

existing albums

1. When you see an album, select a video or a photo to see it in full screen.

2. Click on .

3. Delete the item from only the album or you can remove it from iCloud Photos across all of your devices.

How to rearrange, rename, and delete your existing albums

1. Select the "Albums" tab, and then click on "See All."

2. Choose "Edit," and then carry out any of the actions below;

   - *Rename:* Tap the name of the album, and then input a new name.

   - *Rearrange:* Touch then hold the thumbnail of the album, then drag the album to a different location.

   - *Delete:* Click on ⊖.

   Click on "Done" once you are satisfied.

You will not be able to delete Albums - such as People, Places and Recents – that were created for you by Photos.

How to sort photos in albums

Photos and videos in albums can be sorted by newest to oldest and vice versa. To do this, follow the prompts below;

1. Click on the "Albums" tab, and then choose an album.

2. Select •••, and then click on "Sort."

How to filter photos in your albums

Videos and photos in your album can be filtered by photos, videos, edited and favorites. To carry out this;

1. Click on the "Albums" tab, and then choose an album.
2. Select •••, and then click on Filter.
3. Choose the way you wish to filter your videos and photos in the album and then click on "Done."

If you decide to remove a filter from your album, select ≡, choose "All Items," and then select "Done."

Organize albums in folders

Multiple albums can be contained in a folder. For instance, you can make a folder named "Holidays" and then proceed to create multiple albums within that folder of all your Holidays. Folders can also be created inside another folder. To organize your album;

1. Select the "Albums" tab, and then click on +.

2. Select New Folder.

3. Input a suitable name for the folder, and choose "Save."

4. Tap on the folder to open it, then click on + to create new folders or albums inside the folder.

Share photos and videos on iPhone

Photos and videos can be shared in Messages, mails or some other installed apps by using the Photos app . Photos can even mark some of your best shots from an event and then recommends people you may want to share the picture with.

Share photos and videos

- *Share a single photo or video:* Open the video or photo, click on ⬆️, and then choose how you wish to share the photo or video.

- *Share multiple photos or videos in All Photos or Days:* When you are viewing your photos by All Photos or Days, you can tap on "Select," and then select the photos that you wish to share. Click on ⬆️, and then select a share option. To share all of your images from a day, click on ••• , and then select Share Photos.

  If you turn on iCloud Photos, you can share multiple photos with an iCloud link. The iCloud links can only be active remain for a period of 30 days, and can be accessed by anyone and shared on any app.

- *Share multiple videos or photos in Months:* While you are seeing events by Months, click on ••• , then click on "Share Photos" if you wish to share all of your photos from that particular event.

Shared album can also be used to share videos and pictures with only the people you selected.

Note: Each attachment you want to send has a size limit, which will be determined by your service provider. Live photos are always shared as a still photo on devices that don't support live photos.

Share photos with Sharing Suggestions

Sharing Suggestions suggests a set of pictures from a particular event that you may wish to share and, whom you may wish to share the images with based on the individuals in the photos. Once you share the photos, the individuals that receive the photos will be asked to share their pictures from the same events with you too. Sharing Suggestions will need you to turn on the **iCloud photos** to share, but anyone will be able to see the photos you share.

1. Select the "For You" tab, and then click on a photo collection in the Sharing Suggestions.

2. Click on "Select" to add or remove any photo and then select "Next."

   Photos will suggest that you share the images you took with those who were also present at the event. You can decide on whom to share the picture with, and also add others.

3. Select "Share" in Messages.

   - If you want to share the link with more friends, or to cease sharing, click on the collection, select ⊙, and then select "Copy iCloud Link" or "Stop Sharing."

- If you wish to delete a photo collection from your Sharing Suggestions, select ⊙ , and then click on "Remove Sharing Suggestion."

Save or share a photo or video you receive

- *From email:* Click on the photo or video to download (if needed) and then click on ⬆. Or alternatively touch and hold the file, video or image, then select a saving or sharing option.

- *From a text message:* Click on the video or photo in the chat, click⬆, and then select a saving or sharing option.

CHAPTER THREE

TECHNIQUES FOR RETOUCHING YOUR PHOTOS

It is obvious, at least from the previous chapters, that the iPhone 12 camera can be used to take amazing videos and photos – videos and photos that can be match what can be obtained otherwise with the digital camera. However, due to the nature of snapping photos with mobile camera; the spontaneous nature and the spur-of-the-moment nature of shooting and recording videos, there are errors that are bound to occur during this process. When you bring out your iPhone to record a scene or event, it is possible you have issues relating to composition, light and color. These problems can be fixed with the default Photo apps on your device, and you can even access more advanced capabilities by downloading a wide range of photo and video editing apps from the App store.

In this chapter, you are going to learn how to fix some of the basic photography issues that might arise from iPhone camera usage.

Fix a Photo's Colors

Tools needed: *Photos app and Adobe Light-room app*

A main issue when snapping photos with your device's camera is poor lighting, which can actually result in bad color conditions for the picture. This is not something you can really avoid while taking pictures with the iPhone camera since you might need to use external light sources and instruments to fix it. So, when using iPhone camera, you may have to edit the color for the picture as this is one of the cheapest troubleshooting methods to get the right color for your picture. Basic color editing can be in form of changing a photo property, such as contrast, saturation, temperature, hue etc. There are many photo-editing applications that can allow you to edit the color settings for your photo. In this section, you will see how you can actually modify your image colors with the Photos app on your device and with the Adobe Lightroom app that you can actually download from the App Store free of charge.

Modify Colors Using the Photos App

With the latest updates of the iPhone's iOS, your Photos app now has basic photo modification tools that can allow you to modify your images without necessarily needing to download and install any third party editing software on your phone. The tools in the Photo App can actually provides basic editing capabilities if you don't need much editing for your picture. Proceed with the steps below to edit your pictures with the Photo App;

1. Launch the Photo App from the home screen and select the picture that you wish to edit to show it in full size.
2. Tap on the adjustment icon at the bottom of your screen (looks like three horizontal slider line beside the trash

icon at the bottom of the Photo App's screen). This enables you to use photo-editing mode, as shown below;

3. Tap on the editing icon, as shown below, to bring the edit options for Light, Color, and B&W. The Light options will enable you to modify the light in your picture; the Color will allow you to modify the properties of the color, while the B&W will allow you to convert your photo to black and white.

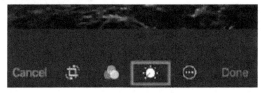

4. Tap on the Color heading to expand it and access more functionality.
5. You can increase the colors saturation by dragging the Saturation slider to the left.

6. Tap on the icon at the top right of the color heading, and choose Contrast in the Color section.
7. Increase the color of the contrast by dragging the slider to the left.

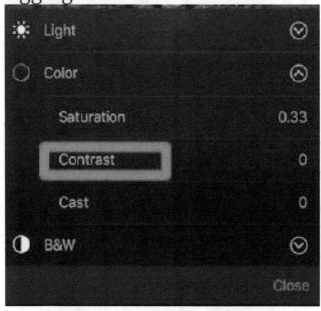

Remove Photo Casting

The light conditions in the surrounding where you are taking your pictures usually affect the color of your photos creating a color casting effect. This occurs most times when you are shooting your photos in some light conditions, like taking pictures in fluorescent light, on cloudy days or in warm light. The color casting effect can distort the clear and natural color in your photo. In another way, you may even wish to use a cast color to bring some special effects in your photo, for instance, adding a warmer tone to your photo. Use the steps below to remove or ad a color cast in your photo;

- Select the adjustment icon (looks like three horizontal slider line beside the trash icon at the bottom of the Photo App's screen) in your Photo App, and choose the Color section.
- Tap on the icon located at the top right section of the color slider.
- Select "Cast" in the Color section heading as shown below;

4.   Create a warmer effect by dragging the slider to your left and a cooler effect will be achieved when you drag the slider to the left as shown in the image below;

5.   Tap **"Done"** when you are satisfied with the result.

Make a Color Adjustment Using Adobe Lightroom

Adobe Lightroom is one of the most popular and powerful application for your photo editing and photo management. It provides advanced capabilities that can be used for modifying your photo and the details of the photo. It is most commonly deployed by professional photographers and people who specialize in photo editing. You will be able to download version of this app on your device from the App Store. A free Adobe ID is needed to utilize this application and you can always create one on the app. The free Adobe Lightroom version will allow users to shoot, arranged, and share pictures from their mobile phones. In fact, with an Adobe Creative Cloud membership, you will be able to use the extended features of the Adobe Lightroom application, and you can even save the source format allowing you to work with both the desktop and mobile version.

The Lightroom app only gives you basic adjustment functionality if you signed up on the app with a free account. In this section, you will learn how to use the Adobe Lightroom app for iPhone to edit your photos. The first thing you need to do is to download and install the Lightrom mobile app from the App Store. Once the app has been successfully installed, launch the app from the Home screen.

Panel in Loupe view

On your iPhone 12, when you select a photo in the Loupe view of your Lightroom for mobile (iOS), you will see that there are more than one panel to work with. But the **Edit panel** will be used in this example;

Edit panel

In the **Edit panel,** you will be able to edit your photo manually using various slider controls like the White Balance, Exposure, Temperature, Contrast, and lots more. You will also be able to crop your images and selectively edit some areas of your picture.

Apply Selective Edit

Selective edit controls from the **Edit** panel can be leveraged to do corrections to a certain part of your photo. For instance, you may wish to lighten the face to let it stand out in the portrait. To do some local corrections, adjustments can be applied by deploying one of the selection tools below;

- The **Brush Selection** tool will allow you mark specific areas of a picture by brushing over them and use adjustments like Exposure, Brightness, Clarity, and other to the marked part of the image.

- The **Radial Selection** ⬡ tool allows you to selectively use adjustments like Exposure, Brightness, Clarity, and other to a specific region of your photo. The shape and dimension of that specific region can also be controlled with the Radial selection tool.
- The **Linear Selection** ⬡ tool will allow you to use these adjustments stealthily across a part of a photo. The area can be made as wide or as narrow as you can.
- The **Depth Selection** ⬡ tool enables you to quickly change a depth map into a selection that you can modify with a brush. This tool specifically works for only HEIC photos with depth map information that was captured with Lightroom's in-app camera (Depth Capture mode) or some other tools for capturing images. To utilize this selection tool, you will need to enable **Depth Mask Creation** located under **Technology Previews** in the app Settings.

  Selective edits will not destroy your photo and are not usually applied permanently on your photo. To apply selective edit, follow the steps below;

1. From the **Edit** panel in the app Loupe view, choose **Selective** icon located at the lower end of your screen.
2. Click on the '**+**' sign that shows at the upper-left corner and then select any of the selective edit tools that you want to deploy - ▨ **Brush Selection**, ◎ **Radial Selection**, ▦ **Linear Selection**, or ▧ **Depth Selection**.
3. Click on the picture to see the selection overlay. The following selective editing tools can be used;

Brush Selection ▨

There are six icons to the left of the selected Brush editing tools. The first icon is called **Brush,** second icon is the **Eraser,** the third icon is the **Size,** the fourth one is called **Feather,** the fifth one is called **Flow** while the last icon is the **Delete selection** tool.

• If you want to move and position the Blue pin you see in the screenshot above, simply drag the Blue pin showing in the middle of the picture.

- Erase the chosen brush selection area with the Eraser tool.
- If you wish to modify the size, feather, or flow of the Eraser or Brush Selection, simply click on the corresponding control from your left, and quickly adjust the value by dragging up or dragging andown on your screen.

✓ **Size**. Indicates the brush's tip dia-meter in pixels.
✓ **Feather**. Do a simple soft-edged trans-ition between the surrounding pixels and the brushed area.

✓ **Flow**. Controls the rate with which you are applying all of the adjustments.

Note:

The red masking is showing the region where the selective edits will be used. You can remove the red masking, if you want, by long pressing the Blue pin showing at the middle of the picture and select "**Never Show Red Overlay.**"

Linear Selection

You will be able to use the Linear selection tools to carry out the selective edits.

- If you wish to move and position the Blue pin you see in the screenshot below, simply drag the Blue pin showing in the middle of the picture.
- The overlay's angle can be adjusted by touching and rotating the white line in the middle of the overlay.
- Expand the effect at a specific end of the spectrum by touching and dragging any of the white lines outside toward the edge of your picture. In the same vein,

you can contract the effect at a particular end of the spectrum by dragging the white line toward the middle of the picture.

- You can utilize the Eraser tool to clean the chosen area of selection.

Note:

The red masking is showing the region where the selective edits will be used. The red masking can be removed (if you wish) by long pressing the Blue pin showing at the middle of the picture and select "**Never Show Red Overlay.**"

Radial Selection ⚙

- Drag the Blue pin in the middle of the overlay to move and position the overlay on the picture.

- Adjust the shape and the size by dragging the white pins on the right, left, and bottom of the picture overlay.

- The **Feather** of your radial selection can be adjusted as you wish by deploying the feather control icon at the left. This is usually done by dragging up or dragging down on the image screen. The percentage of the Feather value is shown at the top section of your screen as you drag.

- The edits just outside of the radial selection overlay can be applied by tapping on the ◨ icon located at the left. Click on the icon again to toggle.

- The chosen selection area can be erased by using the Eraser tool.

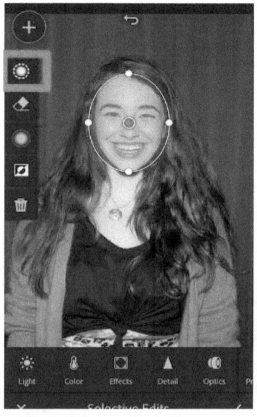

Depth Selection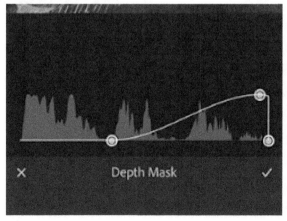

✓ Use the white control pins to edit the Depth Mask by dragging the white control pin just across the depth map.

✓ Click on the 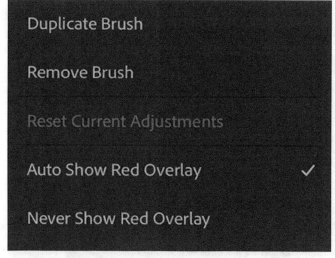 icon located at the top to apply it to the depth mask selection. Click on the icon once again to toggle.

4. A selection overlay can be removed or duplicated by long pressing the Blue pin at the middle of the selection overlay, and then select the necessary options from the displayed pop-up menus.

Duplicate Brush

Remove Brush

Reset Current Adjustments

Auto Show Red Overlay ✓

Never Show Red Overlay

5. Once you have appropriately used the **Brush Selection**, **Linear Selection**, **Radial Selection,** or **Depth Selection** overlay to your satisfaction, select any of the edit

tiles located at the lower end of the screen —choose from **Light**, **Effects**, **Color**, **Details**, and **Optics**. Apply edits on a region of your picture by using the slider in the pop-up menu.

6. Use one finger to tap and hold on your picture to get a "**Before**" view.

To finish the edits, click on ✅ icon.

How to remove unnecessary spots and any unwanted objects in your picture

The **Healing Brush** tools highlighted above can be used to remove any unnecessary spots, objects, people, power lines, or some other side distractions in your picture.

1. From the **Edit** panel in your lightroom app (Loupe view), select the **Healing** icon located at the lower end of your screen as shown above.

2. You can then proceed to use any of the following **Healing Brush** tools:

○ **Heal**: Brings the texture from the source area and then matches it to the tone and color of the target region in your photo.
○ **Clone**: Apply the same pixels from the source region in your photo to the target area.

Both the **Heal** and **Clone** tools use the texture taken from the source area and apply it to the target area. The **Heal** tool, however, takes the tones and colors that surround the target area and then blend all of these together, while the **Clone** actually produces the pixels from the source section to the target area.

A. = Heal B. = Clone C. = Size D. = Feather E. = Opacity F. = Delete G. = Target area H. = Source area I. = hide screen controls to view the photo edits.

By selecting the **Heal (A)** or **Clone (B)** tool above, you can brush over the item in your image that you wish to delete or retouch. Once you have brushed over the item in the picture, you will see two marquee areas. One of the white marquee areas over the painted object indicates the target area, while the second white marquee area that has arrow pointing at the target area indicates the source area.

You can then proceed to modify the size, feather, or opacity of the chosen **Healing** tool as appropriate.

- ✓ **Size**. Indicates the brush's tip diameter in pixels.
- ✓ **Feather**. Do a simple soft-edged transition between the surrounding pixels and the brushed area in the target area.
- ✓ **Opacity**. Adjust the opacity of any adjustment you applied to the target area. Touch the left controls, and then

adjust the value by dragging up or down on the screen.

3. If you desire to move and as well position the source or target area on your photo, simply drag the blue pin at the middle of that area. Click on the (🖾) icon located at the upper-right corner to see the photo edits on a fullscreen. This will hide the screen controls at the bottom and the white source/target areas.

Healing options

Access the **Healing options** by long pressing on the blue pin found just at the center of the source area or the target area to see the **Healing Options** context-menu:

- ✓ From the context-menu, select **Heal** or **Clone** to navigate between the tools.
- ✓ **Delete**: Deletes the chosen source-target area pair.
- ✓ **Reset Healing Brush**: Resets and removes all of the recent adjustments you have made with the **Healing** tools.

4. Long-press on your picture to view a "**Before**" view. To confirm your edits, simply click on  icon.

Crop photos

1. From the **Edit** panel in the Loupe view, select the "**Crop**" icon located at the lower end of your screen.

2. The available Cropping options will be shown as tiles just along the lower end of your screen. You can explore all of the tiles by swiping to the right or left. Click on a tile to use the corresponding option.

3. For extra options, carry out any of the following;

    ○ Click on the Aspect ratio tile to choose one of the cropping aspect ratios. the

- Click on the Aspect **Locked** tile to crop the image without a preset aspect ratio.

- You can straighten the image automatically by clicking on **Straighten** tile.

- Rotate the picture anticlockwise (90 degrees) by tapping on the **Rotate L** tile.

- Rotate the picture clockwise (90 degrees) by tapping on the **Rotate R** tile.

- Horizontally flip the image by tapping on the **Flip H** tile.

- Vertically flip the image by tapping on the **Flip V** tile.

- You can change the size and shape of the crop by dragging the corners and edges of the crop.

- Crop the image by a particular degree by dragging the cropping wheel.

Use one finger to tap and hold on the picture to access a "**Before**" view. You can confirm your edits by tapping on ☑ icon.

Working with preset on your photo

With a **Preset,** you will be able to predetermine positions of selected sliders or all of the sliders and then use them in your photo. Also, you will be able to edit an image to your taste and save the entire slider position so that you can use on other photos.

How to Apply Presets

1. From the **Edit** panel in the Loupe view, select "**Presets**" icon located at the lower end of the screen.

2. You will see the available presets as **Color**, **B&W**, **Creative**, **Curve**, **Sharpening**, **Grain**, and **Vignetting**. Select from any group to access the corresponding Presets. Tap on any Preset to use the preset on your photo.

Note: Transferring user-created presets from the desktop Lightroom Classic to mobile Adobe Photoshop is not possible.

3. Use any of your finger to tap and then hold on the picture to access a "**Before**" view.

To finish the edits, click on ☑ icon.
Select the ⟳ Redo icons or ↺ Undo icons to go forward or move backward one step at a time in your edit.

How to create preset for a user

1. Launch a photo in the Loupe view exactly where you are going to be creating a user preset. Carry out any of the actions below;
   - In the Loupe view, click on the three-dots (⬝⬝⬝) icon located at the upper-right side of your screen to access the options menu. Then, select "Create Preset."
   - From the Edit panel in the Loupe view, click on "Presets icon" located at the lower end of your screen, and then tap on the three-dots (⬝⬝⬝) icon from the

upper-right side of the Presets pop-up screen and tap "Create Preset."

2. Indicate the following in the New Preset screen;

   a. Preset Name: Enter the desired name for the preset.

   b. Preset Group: Custom preset are, by default, saved in the User Presets group. A new group can as well be created with the "New preset" group option.

- Now choose which edit settings you desire to save as a preset.

- Click on the Select pop-up menu and then select any of the following options:

a. All: This will select all of the edit settings groups.

b. Modified: This will only choose the edits settings you have applied on your selected photo.

c. Default: This will select the default set of the edit settings. The features; Tools,

Geometric settings and Optics are, by default, excluded.

d. None: Choosing this implies that you are not planning to select any edit settings.

If you wish to select or deselect some settings manually, click on the check boxes beside the edit setting groups. You can as well tap on the (>) icon to work within the edit setting group, and then select specific settings from the submenu. For instance, you can move within the *Light* settings group and then select/deselect one or even all of the available settings from the submenu - *Exposure, Tone Curve, Contrast, Shadows, Highlights, Whites, and Blacks*.

1. Once you have successfully choose the needed edit settings, click on **Save** located at the upper right section.

The new preset you have created will now be available in the **Preset** menu.

How to delete or update a user preset

1. From the **Edit** panel in the Loupe view, simply tap on the **Presets** icon located at the lower end of the screen.
2. Find the user preset that you plan to delete or update from the Presets pop-up menu. Click on the three-dots (⚬⚬⚬) icon located next to the user preset and select one of the following available options:

Update with Current Settings: From the **Update Preset** screen, the edit settings you wish to include in the user preset can be modified appropriately. Click on the **Select** pop-up menu and then carry out any of the actions below;

- ✓ **All**: This will select all of the edit settings groups.

- ✓ **Default**: This will select the default set of edit settings. It can be any of Tools, Geometry settings and Optics.

- ✓ **None**: This implies you are selecting nothing at all.

If you want to select or deselect some settings manually, click on the check boxes beside the edit setting groups. You can as well tap on the (>) icon to work within the edit setting group, and then select specific settings from the submenu. For instance, you can move within the *Light* settings group and then select/deselect one or even all of the settings from the submenu - *Exposure, Tone Curve, Contrast, Shadows, Highlights, Whites, and Blacks*.

Save: Once you have successfully modify the required edit settings, click on **Save** at the upper right section.

Rename: You will be able to modify **Preset Name** as appropriate from the **Rename Preset** screen. Once you have modified the preset name, click on **"Save"** at the upper-right side.

Delete: You will be able to delete the user preset permanently by choosing this option.

How to manage presets

The **Manage Presets** option will allows you to hide or show various preset groups shown in the Presets menu - **Color**, **B&W**, **Creative**, **Curve**, **Sharpening**, **Grain**, **Vignetting** and **User Presets**.

You can as well use the **Manage Presets** option to display the legacy Lightroom preset groups, which are usually hidden by default.

Follow the steps below to show or hide the preset group;

1. From the **Edit** panel in the Loupe view, click on **Presets** icon located at the lower end of the screen.
2. Click on the icon that looks like three-dots (⚬⚬⚬) located at the upper-right end of your screen and click on **Manage Presets**.
3. When you are right within the **Manage Presets** screen, you can toggle on the specific preset groups that you wish to display in the Presets menu. Toggle off the preset groups that you plan to hide from your Presets menu.

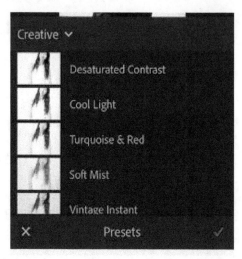

When you are satisfied, select "**Done**" at the upper-right end.

How to hide presets that are partially compatible

From the **Presets** panel, you will be able to access specific presets in italics because they are partially compatible presets. This implies that the profiles that are associated with these presets are meant for another camera. These presets can be hidden in the presets panel. If you want to conceal all presets that are not compatible with your current picture, follow the steps below;

1. Tap a photo to open in Loupe view and select **Preset** from the **Edit** panel.

2. Click on the icon that looks like three-dots located at the upper-right end in the **Presets** panel to access the options menu.
3. Click on "**Show Partially Incompatible**" to turn it off. You will no longer be able to see partially incompatible presets in the preset panel.

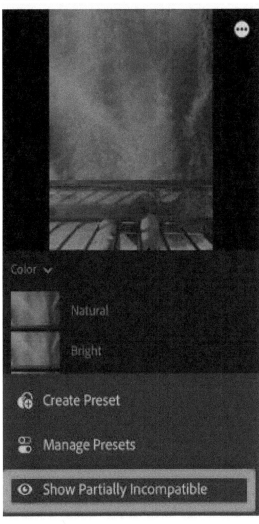

Adjust the tonal scale of a photo

You can use the tone controls in the **Light** menu to adjust the tonal level of photos. To do this, follow the steps below;

1. From the **Edit** panel, click on **Light** icon from the lower end of your screen to see the tone controls.
2. Though optional, you can select **Auto** to adjust the entire tonal scale. Adobe Photoshop Lightroom will set the slider automatically to minimize any unwanted shadows and highlights and maximize the entire scale.

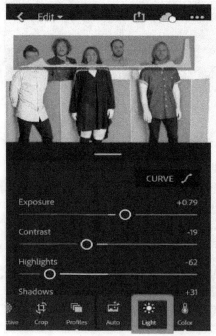

3. Adjust the tone control sliders:

Note:

You can use two fingers to tap on the image to bring the histogram. Start looking at the histogram while you work to adjust the image's tone control to see what is really happening.

From the tone control slider, the following settings can be adjusted;

Exposure

Adjust the total brightness for the photo. Start adjusting the brightness slider until you are satisfied with the appearance of the picture and until you get the intended image brightness.

Contrast

Increases or reduces the image contrast, majorly affecting the midtones. When you raise the contrast, the middle-to-dark image parts will become darker, and the middle-to-light image parts will actually become lighter. As you reduce the contrast, the tones of the image are affected inversely.

Highlights

This can be used to modify areas in the photo that are bright. You can drag the white circle (check the screenshot above) to your left hand side to darken highlights and also to recover "blown out" highlight details. You will be able to brighten the highlights by dragging the white circle across the highlights slider to brighten the highlights.

Shadows

This is used to provide adjustments to dark image areas. Drag the white circle on the shadow slider to the left hand side to darken shadows. The white circle can also be dragged to the right hand side to brighten shadow areas and to recover shadow details.

Whites

This can be used to modify any white clipping. Drag the white circle to the left hand side to decrease the clipping in highlights. Drag the white circle to your right hand side to increase highlight clipping.

Blacks

This is used to modify black clippings. Drag the white circle to the left to increase black clipping and Drag the white circle to the right to decrease the shadow clipping.

How to Fine-tune the tonal scale using the

Tone Curve

From the **Light** menu, the **Tone Curve** graph stands for any changes you made to the entire tonal scale of your image.

From the **Edit** panel, click on the **Light** icon located at the lower end of your screen and then select **CURVE** 🖊 icon to see the **Tone Curve** graph overlay over your photo.

The horizontal axis indicates the actual tone values (the values you input). You will be able to see black values to the left side and the values become progressively lighter toward the right. The vertical axis indicates the changed tone values (output values), showing black at the bottom and the values become progressively lighter tending to white as it gets to the top. The tone curve, essentially, is used to modify any previous tone adjustments you made to an image.

You can as well decide to carry out some minor adjustments to each points on the tone curve in the Blue, Red, or Green channel individually, or on all of the three channels at once.

✓ Tap once to add a point, and tap twice to remove a point.

✓ Edit a point by dragging the point.

How to adjust color in your image

The **Color** menu is found to the right of the **Light** menu at the bottom of the Loupe view Edit screen. From the **Edit** panel, you can leverage the **Color** menu to carry out the following tasks;

• **White Balance** is the color that was created in your image using the temperature of your source of light. For instance, the sunlight on a noonday might cast a warm, yellow color on your photo whereas many light bulbs will usually cast a cool, blue color in your photo. Use the **White balance selector** to specify a neutral area in your image or set your **White Balance** by selecting a preset option.

- The white balance can be further fine-tuned by using the **Temp** and **Tint** controls. **Temp** or Temperature is the one that will set how yellow/warm or how blue/cool your image will looks. **Tint**, on the other hand will sets how magenta or green your picture will look.

- Utilize the **Vibrance** and **Saturation** controls to adjust the saturation (vividness) of the color. **Vibrance** will increase the strength/power of muted colors while **Saturation** will increase the strength/power of all of the colors in your image.
- Black and White photography is a useful tool of professional photographers to allow viewers to drive into the photo's details. The **B&W** option can be used to convert the image to black and white.

- Utilize the **Hue**, **Saturation**, and **Luminance** (HSL) slider to further fine-tune each color. the **Hue** will adjusts the tone of each color, the **Saturation** will adjusts the level of gray in a color hence making the color to be more muted or bright and the **Luminance** will help to adjust the level of white in a color to enable it looks darker or brighter. The **Target Adjustment** tool can be used to adjust a specific color in your photo. Simply tap on the photo and then drag to modify the color range.

- If you have the latest Lightroom for mobile (iOS) version 6.0, the colors of midtones, highlights and shadows can be adjusted with the **Color Grading** sliders. A **Global** slider is also available, with which you will be able to adjust the whole colors in your photo without necessarily affecting the midtones, highlights and shadow settings. In addition, you will be able to adjust the **Balance, Luminance**, and **Blending** of the colors for midtones, highlights and shadows by using their sliders.

How to apply effects in your images

1. From the **Edit** panel in the Loupe view, select **Effects** icon located at the lower end of the screen to bring the controls.
2. Adjust the effects sliders under the following;

Texture

Accentuates or smoothens the textured details in your picture. You can smoothen the details by moving the slider to your left, while you can accentuate details by moving the slider to the right. Adjusting the **texture** slider will not affect the tonality or color.

Clarity

When you increase the local contrast, you will be able to add more depth to your photo. To maximize this effect, try to increase the setting until you notice halos near the edge details of your photo. And you can then proceed to slightly reduce the settings. When you are using this setting, it is better you zoom in the picture to 100% or higher. To zoom in, simply tap twice on the picture or you can even zoom in by using the outward spread gesture.

Dehaze

The level of haze in a picture can be controlled with Dehaze. Remove haze by dragging ti the right, while you will need to drag to the left to add haze.

Vignette Amount

For artistic effect, you can add a light or dark vignette to your photo. The corners of the picture become darken with negative values while the corner becomes lighten with positive values.

Grain

This can help you to add film-grain effect that is realistic to your image. You can add grain by dragging the slider to the right hand side. After adding grain, the roughness of the grain and the size of the grain can be controlled with the **Roughness** and **Size** slider respectively.

How to use Noise reduction to get your photos sharpened

In the Adobe Photoshop Lightroom app for iPhone, you will be able to sharpen your picture to achieve enhance edge definition and further bring out more details in your photo. Image noise can be reduced when you remove the extraneous obvious artifacts that reduce the quality of an image. Image noise can include luminance noise (grayscale) – which makes your image appears grainy, and color noise – which normally appear as colored artifacts in your picture. Images you shot using high ISO may have glaring noise. To apply Noise reduction, follow the steps below;

From the **Edit** panel, click on **Detail** icon located at the lower end of your screen.

Pictures can be sharpened at two stages; when you view and edit images and when you export or print images. Sharpening is an essential part of the camera default, which is usually applied to your images.

1. From the Develop module, simply zoom in on your photo to about 100% or more.
2. Drag in the Navigator panel to check an area of the image that highlights the sharpening adjustment effect.
3. You will be able to adjust any of these sharpening tools from the Detail panel;

Amount

This will adjusts edge definition. You can increase sharpening by increasing the value. If you input a value of zero (0), you will be able to turn off sharpening completely. To achieve a cleaner picture, use a lower value.

Radius

Adjusts the details size that sharpening is applied to. Pictures with very fine details may require a smaller radius setting. Pictures with larger details may use a larger radius. When you use radius that is too large, you will get a picture that look unnatural.

Detail

You will be able to set how much high-frequency information should be sharpened in your image and how much the sharpening process should emphasize the edges. A Lower setting will sharpen edges to take out blurring. Higher values make the texture in your photo to be more pronounced.

Masking

This is used to set an edge mask. With a value of zero (0), everything in your picture gets equal amount of sharpening. With a value of 100, sharpening will be restricted mostly to those parts that are near to the strongest edges.

How to correct common camera lens flaws

Camera lenses can have various types of defects at some focal lengths, focus distances and f-stops. The **Optics** option can be used to automatically adjust the apparent camera lens distortion.

1. From the **Edit** panel, click on **Optics** icon located at the bottom of the edit screen.
2. Chromatic aberration usually appears as a color fringe along the objects' edges. It is mostly a result of the lens inability to focus different colors to a single spot, flare and aberrations in the sensor microlenses.

Chromatic Aberration: Toggle this to ON to correct red-green fringes and blue-yellow in your photo.

Enable Lens Correction: Toggle to ON to use lens correction on your picture.

How to Copy and paste edits

If you have the Adobe Lighroom version 5.0 and above, you will be able to copy, edits you have applied to a particular picture and then paste them to multiple pictures you have selected. To get started;

1. Tap a picture to open the picture in Loupe view.

2. Tap on the three-dots (⚬⚬⚬) icon located in the upper-right corner and select **Copy Settings**.

3. From the **Copy Settings** panel, choose the edits that you wish to copy. You can choose edit setting groups like Profile: Tool, Color, Light, etc. Optionally, you can tap on the **Select** drop-down list to select one of these;

- **All**: Tapping on this will select all of the edit settings groups.
- **Modified**: This will only select the edits settings that you have already modified or that you have applied on the chosen photo.
- **Default**: This will select the default edit settings. Tools settings and Geometry settings are by default excluded.
- **None**: This will un-select all of the edit settings.

  You can as well decide to select or un-select some settings in each edit setting group. Click on the arrow icon on each edit setting group to see its specific settings.

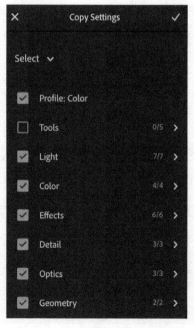

Once you have made all your selections, click on the ☑ icon.

From the grid view of your desired album or of "**All Photos,**" choose the pictures that you wish to paste the settings you have copied to.

Note:
If you only have just one image that you want to paste the settings you have copied to, open your image in Loupe view, click on the (▥) icon, and select "**Paste Settings.**"
Select **Paste** from the bottom panel.
You will be prompted with a Paste Settings confirmation dialog box where you can click on **"Apply."** The copied settings will then be applied to the chosen photos.

Note:
Alternatively, you can follow the method below to copy default settings of a photo you have edited from the Grid view in an album or **"All Photos."**

1. Choose the edited photo in Grid view.

2. Select **Copy** from the bottom panel to copy your default edit settings of the photo you selected.

3. Tap on all of the photo(s) in the grid to which you plan to paste the settings you have copied to.

4. Click on **Paste** from the bottom panel. Select "**Apply**" from the confirmation dialog.

How to create edit version

Versions allow you to quickly save various edits of the same picture so that you will be able to experiment with editing and make comparism between two or more edits. To make a version;

1. Open an image in **Edit** view and use the desired edits.

2. Navigate the bottom panel and select **Versions**.

3. You can access the **Original, which** is the real picture you imported. If any editing has been made to the picture, you will be able to view those modifications under the **Current** section. Select **"Create Version"** if you want to save the current edits as a Version.

4. Input a desired name for the Version and select **Create**. Doing this will allow you to use different edits and save those edits as versions.

5. Choose a **Version** and click on the three-dot icon to delete or rename the version.

Note:

- The **Versions** you are synced across Lightroom desktop and Lightroom for mobile (iOS and Android).

- As at the Lightroom for mobile version 6.0, significant edits of your images are saved by the **Versions** panel as a **Version.** You will be able to access the automa-tically saved **Versions** anytime you carry out a significant edit, leave the **Edit** view and then go back to the **Versions** panel.

How to send your photos to Photoshop on

iPad

This feature was designed with the intro-duction of the Lightroom for iPad version 5.3

1.   From the Lightroom app on your iPad, click on the desired photo and select the **Share** icon.

2.   Tap **Edit in Photoshop**.

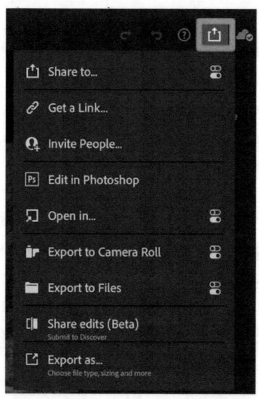

2.   Do your edits in Photoshop on your iPad.

To transfer the photo back to the Lightroom app, choose **Send to Lightroom** from the top panel.

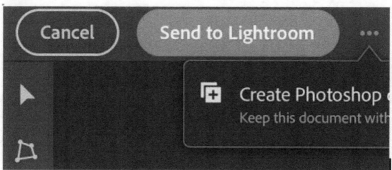

CHAPTER FOUR

HANDY PHOTOGRAPHY AND VIDEO ACCESSORIES FOR THE iPhone 12

Most photographers and professional video-graphers have resorted to using their iPhone camera to take amazing shots and record cinema worthy videos. This is because most of the conventional digital cameras like the DSLR, Camcorders etc are very expensive. With the iPhone camera, it has now becomes especially very easy to achieve a powerful cinematographic effect in your pictures and videos. However, just as it is with conve-ntional digital cameras, you can improve the quality of shots and the convenience with which iPhone cameras take pictures and record videos by using accessories with the iPhone camera. These iPhone camera acces-sories help to achieve professionalism in the quality of shots you take with your iPhone camera. It is quite important to say that these camera accessories are affordable and can be afforded by users who enjoy taking amazing moments and upload their cinema worthy videos on YouTube and other social media platforms. Accessories can range from Stabilizers, lens and some other useful accessories.

Find below some affordable iphone accessories that give a professional cinematographic effect;

- **Handheld Gimbal Stabilizer for iPhones**: It might be very difficult to record videos that are particularly non-shaky with your iPhone camera. This is due to the fact that you can barely avoid moving around while taking pictures and recording videos with your iPhone camera. To prevent you from shooting eventually shooting a video that will look blurry in appearance, you can try attaching your iPhone 12 to a stabilizer. One common stabilizer is the **Gimbal**

Stabilizer, which helps to secure your iPhone and hold it in shape to eliminate unwanted shaky motion, which can eventually lead to blurry images during shooting. The **Osmo mobile 3** stabilizer is effective for this purpose. The Osmo mobile 3 is portable, usable with one hand and you can carry it anywhere you are going. Another common stabilizer you can consider is the Feiyutech VLOG pocket. The VLOG pocket features a button that can allow you to switch between landscape mode and portrait mode.

Osmo Mobile 3

- **25X External telephoto zoom lens**: The lenses that accompanied iPhone 12, although very powerful, can be complemented with an external lens to produce very powerful cinematic and quality videos and images. The normal telephoto lens is good but it is advisable you go for the dual type. The lens will usually adjust the distance between its own eyepiece and that of your phone camera making it very easy to shoot without any dark imprints. Use this lens to get a god quality video and pictures from your iPhone camera.

25X External telephoto zoom lens

- **Wide-angle 3-in-1 lens**: The wide-angle lens gives a moderate magnification that can you're your object of shot and makes it have a direct focus on your camera. The fish eye design that accompanies the lens let you give a unique fish eye effect to your photos and videos.

Wide-angle 3-in-1 lens

- **Rode Video Mic Me-L**: The in-built microphone that comes with your phone might not be able to provide the required sound effect, hence it might be okay to attach an external microphone.

The external microphone will offer an improvement to the inbuilt microphone that comes with iphone devices. When coupled with your iphone 12, it gives an adorable sonic sound to your video recordings. The broader range of frequency in the device gives users a wide audible range. The microphone is designed to send out any sound hitting the sides of the microphone. Its directionality only allows it to receive sound from the object to which it is directly pointing toward. It is able to capture high quality audio more than the capacity of the inbuilt microphone

Rode Mic Me-L

- **SandMac Hybrid filter**: This filter improves landscape videography. The filter serves to protect your camera from overexposing itself to light, hence improving the HDR of your camera. The lens also serves to give your video footage a perfect cinematic look.

- **Adonit photogrip QI:** This is a multi-tool device for people who love deploying their iPhone camera to shoot videos. The usefulness lies in the grip itself, which can expand to fit any device with just about any 4.5-inch or larger. The grip carries out many functions. Its main function is to allow users get a good grip of their iPhone. It is also a wireless charger featuring a 3000mAh battery capacity. If you cast it on your wireless-compatible iPhone, your device will still be charging while you will be busy shooting videos. The grip can be charged with either a USB-A or a USB-C cable. It will charge the phone while you're busy recording videos and taking photos. The grip is chargeable with a USB-A or a USB-C type.

- **Beast grip**: You can leverage this to attach many types of filter, standard conversion lenses, photos and video accessories and gears. Furthermore, it provides stability and ease for handheld shots. The beast grip also gives users easy access to their phone buttons, charging ports and USB, superb design with a removable lens mount assembly and handle.

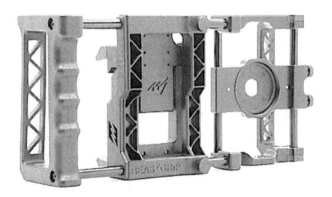

- **Lumu power**: The Lumu is a light meter version on our Smartphones. This device will turn your iPhone into a handheld light and color meter. Lumu works on any iPhone with a lightning port. Connect the Lumu to your gadget, and use it to adjust the lighting condition before taking that shot. The company that designed Lumu has now taken the game to another level. The new Lumu power now has two sides; the color side with a color sensor that measures the color temperature of the camera, white balance and illumination, and another side with a silicone photodiode that measures camera expo-sure, ambient light, and the flashlight.

- **Dimmable selfie light with tripod**: this selfie light will take away all the shadows from your video and let your video appears more cinematic. It is very easy to use.

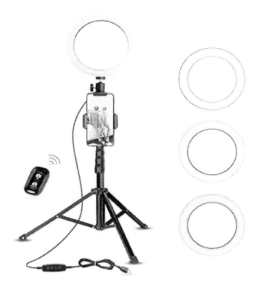

- **Underwater photographer case for iphone 12**: The iPhone 12 is rated IP68 and is designed to stay under water (not more than 2 meters) for not more than 30 minutes. This means that you will be able to record videos under water, especially when you are interested in studying how the ways of live of aquatic organisms. While in water, the underwater videographer case can further serve to protect your iPhone from being affected by water, and you can then conveniently record your video even while in water.

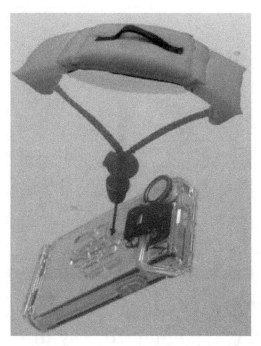

- **Tripod**: This is used to achieve the sharpest possible shot by merely positioning your device camera at a better angle. The Joby Gorillapod hybrid is very portable and durable.

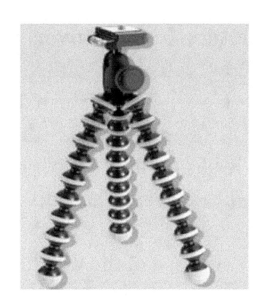

- **Rov Motorized Slider**: You can leverage this to record cinematic movements with your iPhone camera. With a single tap of button, the motorized slider will start moving while seamlessly recording your video in the process.

- **Profoto C1 plus cover**: Control light anyhow you wish with the Profoto C1 Plus cover. This external flashlight is able to synchronize with your iPhone and it has an app, which can only work on iOS devices. The app has a camera feature that is able to directly connect with the flash of the C1 Plus. The Profoto is like an improvisation to the LED light in your phone camera.

iPhone photo editing software

In the previous section, you have seen how the Adobe Lightroom can provide improved functionality for your iPhone camera. While the Adobe Lightroom is probably among the best editing software you can use for achieving great shots with your iPhone camera, there are still other photo and video editing software that can be purchased or downloaded for free on the App Store. The following are editing software you can check out;

✓ **Snapseed:** Available on Android and iOS devices. You can get it on the App store. Best for advanced picture editing. It is free.
✓ **VSCO:** Available on Android and iPhones. It is free.
✓ **Prisma Photo Editor:** Turn your images into paintings and drawings. Available on Android and iOS devices. You can get it on the App store. Best for advanced picture editing. It is free.
✓ **Adobe Photoshop Express:** This is good for overall image editing. Available on Android and iOS devices. You can get it on the App store. Best for advanced picture editing. It is free.

✓ **Foodie:** Take images of your food to the next level. Available on Android and iOS devices. You can get it on the App store. Best for advanced picture editing. It is free.

✓ **Live collage:** Create photo collage. Available on Android and iOS devices. You can get it on the App store. Best for advanced picture editing. It is free.

CHAPTER FIVE

FilMic Pro App for Cinematic video: Getting more than just a video

While most Digital cameras, Smartphone cameras and mirrorless cameras can shoot videos using automatic settings inbuilt in them, it becomes expedient to say that manual settings can aid cinematographers in shooting cinematic worthy videos. Since most iPhone cameras do not have manual settings to further improve the quality of videos, a number of third party apps can be installed on your iPhone 12 to give manual settings control. One of such third party apps that can be downloaded to give your video an edge over what could be otherwise obtainable is the **FilMic Pro.**

The **FilMic Pro** app is very compatible with iPhone 12 and app compatibility should be the least of your worries.

How to set Focus using the FilMic Pro

It is a good observation that the camera needs to be properly focused on the subject if you want to have the subject to be clear in the image. Setting the camera focus actually depends on aperture and the nature of the camera lens. The rule of **Focus** imagined that; a **small aperture + a wide lens = more of the subject in focus,** while a **wider aperture + long lens = less of the subject in focus.** From this illustration, it is clear that a wide lens with a small aperture setting is what is required to get your subject to appear more in the camera. This is normally refers to as **Depth of Field.** A shallow depth of field creates a blurry background. To set the focus in the FilMic Pro, use the icon that looks like white rectangle in the middle of the screen (you will see the icon marked with a green circle. To set **Focus,** you will have to position the white rectangle over the subject you want to focus on. If you want to set your

Focus on another subject/area in the video, simply move the rectangular icon to where the subject is. In the picture below, the focus has been set on the glass.

During professional filming, if you want to make your video appear good enough, you will have to **lock the focus** at one distance by simply tapping on the rectangle and you will see it turning to red (instead of white). When you tap record, the focus will be exactly where you have set it even if the camera is moved or any part of the subject changes position.

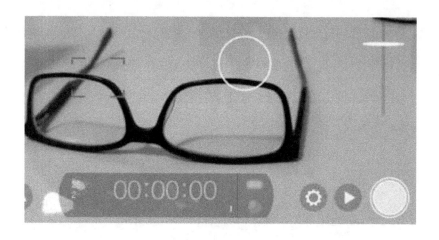

If you want to unlock the focus (so that you will be able to diversify the focus, tap on the red rectangle icon and you will see it turning white again.

How to set Resolution in FilMic Pro

Before you start shooting video, it is important to know which resolution you want to use for the video. The number of pixels that is in one frame of the video is called **Resolution.** Actually, the higher the pixels number, the higher the quality of your video but the higher the size of the video file. Larger resolution also implies high processing power when you are playing the video or applying other video effects. Currently, most Smartphone cameras have been restricted to 4K as the highest resolution. To set the **Resolution** in FilMic Pro,

- Look at the small cogwheel (**settings icon**) at the bottom right of the FilMic Pro interface and tap on the icon. The settings icon has been marked with red in the image below;

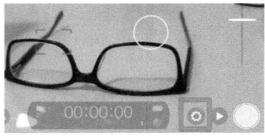

- You will be prompted with the **Settings** menu where you can select **Resolution** as shown below;

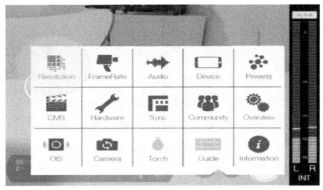

When you tap on the **Resolution** option above, you will get

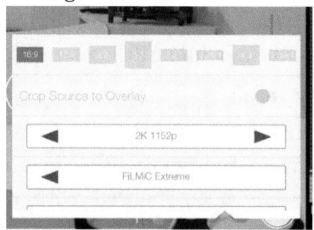

Use the arrow to choose between a number of resolutions. On iPhone 12, the following resolutions are available; 4k 2160p, 3k 1836p, 2k 1152p, HD 1080p and HD 720p. The best resolution for most of your cinematic shootings is the 2160 4k. The 4K shooting gives moderate shot with high quality.

How to choose Aspect ratio

Aspect ratio is the one that will dictate the shape of the video frame. When you look at the screenshot above where you selected your video resolution, you will see the available aspect ratios at the top.

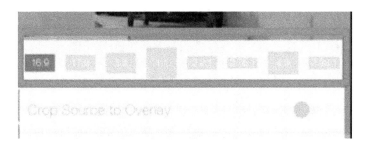

The available aspect ratios in FilMic Pro include; 16:9, 17:9, 3:2, 1:1, 2.2:1, 2.76:1, 4:3, and 2.39:1. Most videos are shot with the 16:9 aspect ratios. The 16:9 aspect ratio is the standard mostly convenient for videos on your iPhones, TVs, and other gadgets. Many TV screens use the 16:9 aspect ratio. When you want to use other aspect ratios that are not the normal 16:9, you need to switch off the "**crop overlay source**."

You can also set your video **Bitrate.** The **Bitrate** control is just below the **resolution** control and you can access more **Bitrates** by tapping on **FilMic Extreme.** The **FilMic Extreme** is the highest Bitrate you can set.

The larger your Bitrate, the more the video quality, but one thing you have to compensate for the high quality is the larger size of the video. In case you are likely to subject the final video to more processing and effects later, you should, then endeavor to use the highest bitrate that your device can actually manage.

How to adjust frame rate on FilMic Pro

The Frame rate refers to the number of frames recorded or played back in a second. Higher frame rate will literally create bigger video size, which, in this case, doesn't necessarily imply high quality shot. There are many frame rates you can select from for your video, which include; 24fps, 25fps, 30fps, 60fps etc.

- If you want to make your video have a **film** like look, then use the frame rate of 24 or 25fps and set the shutter speed to either 1/48 or 1/50. This adjustment will help you add motion blur in your video, which is almost similar to when you are using a film camera.

- The standard for TV is the 30fps, which provides improved video clarity better for sport video and news report. The default setting for most iPhone cameras is to shoot videos at 30fps.
- For slow motion effect is the use of 60fps and higher. Although, the resulting video might look too synthetic and too clear to be a true video.

Note: The artificial light in your room, if matches the frequency of the light bulb, might affect your video and make it contains artificial light flickering on and off on playback. For instance, in the USA, a frame rate of 30fps might matches 60HZ electricity, which is usually supplied.

To adjust the Frame rate in FilMic pro, tap on the **settings** icon and select the **Frame rate** button.

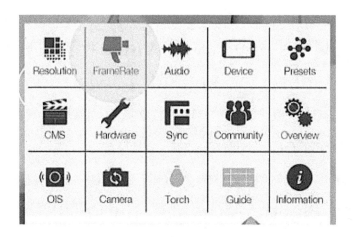

When you tap on the Frame rate menu, a screen will be prompted where you can adjust your frame rate.

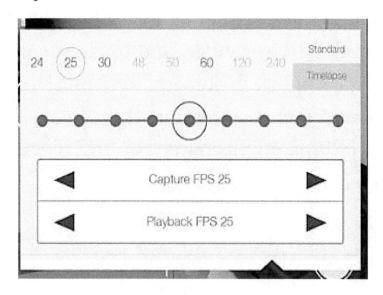

How to adjust Video exposure in FilMic Pro

There are some factors, which usually affect the video exposure all of which usually affect the final outlook of the video. The settings which normally affect video exposure include; **ISO, Shutter speed** and **Aperture.**

- **ISO:** The ISO dictates how sensitive the sensor of your camera will be to light. If the image is dark, you can raise the ISO to let the camera sensor be more sensitive to light. If your image is too bright and you need it to be dark, you can reduce the ISO to get a darker image. As it with your iPhone camera (designed with small sensor not good at getting light in low light conditions), there is a bad side effect when you increase the ISO. The side effect will be in the form of video noise. To reduce video noise, do not set the ISO above 100.

- **Shutter speed:** This refers to how many times the shutter of the camera is opened to allow light come into the sensor. The iPhone camera doesn't come with inbuilt settings to adjust the shutter speed. But with a third party app like the FilMic Pro, you will be able to adjust the shutter speed. A faster shutter speed implies a dark image while a slower shutter speed means a lighter image. You can also use shutter speed to control the level of motion blur in your video. A faster shutter speed gives less blur while a slower shutter gives more blur. Essentially, you can consider the following tips to make your video looks like a film motion blur;

o **High frame rate** with a **faster shutter speed** gives a smooth and a very clear video.

o **Slow shutter speed** with a slow frame rate makes a motion blur with a film look video.

- **Aperture:** This refers to the size of the hole that allows light through the hole in the camera sensor. A small aperture, as you would agree implies less light, which creates deeper depth of focus.

Now, to set the ISO, shutter speed and the Aperture (all of which control exposure settings) in the FilMic pro, click on the circular icon located at the bottom left side of the FilMic Pro App to open the **Manual control.**

When you tap on the circular icon, you will see two wheel controllers at the side. The wheel at the right is for setting focus and zoom while the wheel on the left is for shutter speed and ISO.

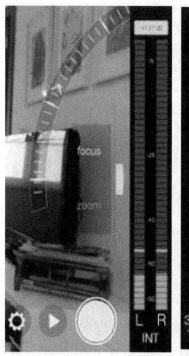

Change the exposure by moving the left slider wheel up and down while you watch your screen going brighter and darker as you adjust. Choose your desired frame rate and shutter speed. If you are in a low light condition, you should try and move the ISO pass 100 or even in some cases 200. If you go beyond this, there may be extra noises in your video.

Setting white balance

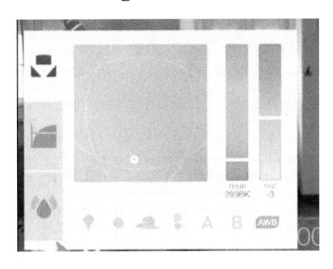

Setting white balance allows you to record colors as precisely as you can with your device's camera. Different light sources come with different color temperatures. Modern digital cameras are now having sensors, which can precisely set white balance automatically. But your video recording can look untidy if the white balance changes by itself automatically during the process. So, to allow you to make cinematic video, the white balance has to be locked. You can first set the white balance by holding a piece of white cloth in front of the camera.

You can set and lock the white balance in the FilMic app by clicking the colored circle icon at the bottom left of the interface and this will launch the white balance control. In case, for one reason or another, you cannot set the white balance, you should at the very least

Tapping on the AWB icon will automatically change the white balance as you change position from one place to another place, of from one lighting condition to another. You can also use the AWB icon to lock the white balance setting (red). Move the white selector inside the color rectangle to adjust the temperature and tints

Setting white balance will eliminate all strange colors in your video making white looks like white and other colors too falling in places.

Recording Videos on the FilMic Pro

Tap on the record button marked in red. Tap the same button again to stop recording.

Device Settings

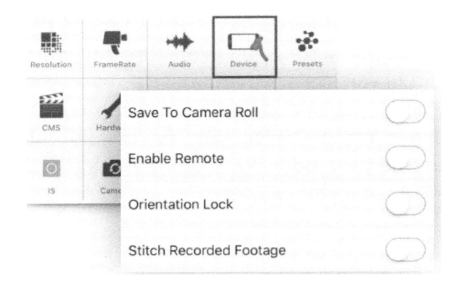

- **Save to Camera Roll:** With this setting, you will be able to save your shots by default to the camera roll. Saving to the App library, rather than the camera roll, might be better if you want to make sure that original video quality is not lost and the file name is maintained as it is. When copying your video to the camera roll, there may be lost of data during the transfer, which might be difficult to get back.

-   **Enable Remote:** You can toggle on this setting if you have linked the FilMic remote with the FilMic Pro app.

- **Orientation Lock:** This setting allows you to keep the current orientation lock of the app. If you are in vertical orientation and you enable this setting, the FilMic Pro app will be kept in vertical orientation.

- **Stitch Recorded footage:** When you are recording live, you can pause and later resume your video coverage, and the clip can be joined together later.

ABOUT AUTHOR

Derrick Richard is a tech geek with several years of experience in the ICT industry. He passionately follows latest tech trends and his passion is in figuring out the solution to complex problems. Derrick found his passion with how camera works when he was a child. His interest in videography has spurred him to harness his skills in creating YouTube videos for people to enjoy. He also teaches beginners how to make videos with mid-range cameras, especially with Smart phones.

Derrick holds a Bachelor and a Master's Degree in ICT respectively from Georgetown University, Washington DC. He lives in Sarasota, Florida.

www.ingramcontent.com/pod-product-compliance
Lightning Source LLC
LaVergne TN
LVHW022124060326
832903LV00063B/3693